Original title: Pathways of Moonlight

Copyright © 2024 Swan Charm Publishing
All rights reserved.

Author: Kaido Väinamäe
Editor: Jessica Elisabeth Luik
ISBN 978-9916-39-977-4

Pathways of Moonlight

Kaido Väinamäe

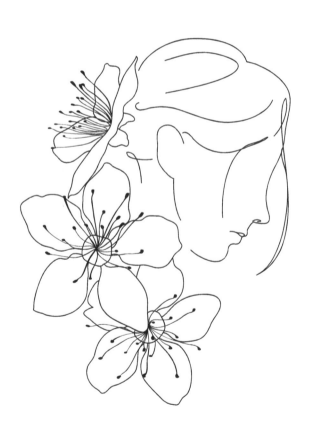

Silvery Routes

Beneath the stars, a path unfolds,
A shimmer in the night so bold.
Journey through the silvery routes,
Where dreams and whispers both take root.

Moonlight bathes the winding track,
Guiding feet that won't look back.
Mysteries of night take flight,
In silvery routes of endless light.

Whispers of the breeze do sing,
Of secrets night does softly bring.
Crafted in the starlight's weave,
On silvery routes, we find reprieve.

Moonbeam Wanderings

Moonbeams dance on rivers fair,
Casting light beyond compare.
Soft reflections in the stream,
We wander through a lunar dream.

Echoes of the night, so grand,
Play on shadows' silent band.
Moonbeam wanderings take flight,
In the velvet hush of night.

Crystal beams paint visions bright,
Whispering tales in silver light.
Through the darkness, hand in hand,
Moonbeam wanderers understand.

Celestial Roads

In the sky, where dreams do roam,
Celestial roads have found their home.
Stardust paths that twist and turn,
Guiding those who stories yearn.

Galaxies in spiral dance,
Invite us with a fleeting glance.
Celestial roads of cosmic plight,
Bridge the heavens with their light.

Silent vastness, grand and fair,
We traverse with earnest dare.
On celestial roads we stray,
Where night meets the break of day.

Twilight Footprints

In twilight's soft and tender hue,
Footprints mark the evening's view.
Paths of dusk, where shadows lay,
Guides of nightfall, lead our way.

Silent steps on twilight's shore,
Echoes of the day before.
Whispered tales in fading light,
Footprints of the early night.

As the stars begin to play,
Twilight footprints gently sway.
Through the dim and quiet dusk,
We walk in twilight's fragrant musk.

Nocturnal Treks

Underneath the moon's soft glow,
Shadows dance in quiet show.
Whispers from the gentle breeze,
Rustling leaves with tender ease.

Stars above with twinkling eyes,
Guide our hearts through darkened skies.
Steps we take on silent ground,
Mystery in each step found.

Crisp the air in velvet night,
Owl's call adds magic light.
Endless realms where dreams reside,
In these paths where night abides.

Footprints fade in starlit mist,
Night and dream forever kissed.
Echoes of the woodland's rest,
Nocturnal treks, souls' quest.

Fleeting moments, time stands still,
In the night's embrace, a thrill.
Journey ends, yet lingers on,
In our hearts, nocturne's song.

Glistening Gosafzi Paths

Dew-kissed blooms in morning's light,
Gosafzi paths, a pure delight.
Whispers of the ancient trees,
Guide us through with gentle ease.

Golden rays and shadows play,
Marking time, both night and day.
Petals soft beneath our feet,
A tranquil world, so discreet.

Birds sing out with joyous sound,
Nature's choir, all around.
Glistening trails of emerald green,
Secrets of the earth unseen.

Each new step, a story told,
Paths alive with dreams of old.
Magical the moment's weave,
In this haven, we believe.

Soft and bright, the path unfolds,
Gosafzi's heart, truth it holds.
Everlasting in our minds,
Where peace and beauty intertwine.

Night Silver Tracks

Moonlight paints the silent rails,
Night silver tracks, wistful tales.
Echoes past in whispers' flight,
Trains of dream in shadowed night.

Ghostly lights in distant gleam,
Merge with land's eternal dream.
Wheels on tracks in hushed refrain,
Songs of journeys, loss, and gain.

Every mark on weathered steel,
Tells of hearts that dare to feel.
Nighttime cloak on rails so fine,
Intertwines with fate's design.

Silent stories fold and blend,
Endless paths that never end.
Time stands still, the world retracts,
Within these night silver tracks.

Morning breaks, the veil will lift,
Tracks remain, an ageless gift.
Journey's end, yet still they call,
Timeless whispers, night enthrall.

Phantom Trails

Silhouettes in moon's soft glow,
Walk the paths of shadowed lore.
Where the phantom breezes blow,
Through the realms of yesteryore.

Whispers in the twilight air,
Calling from a world unseen.
Memories of old despair,
Linger where the stars convene.

Haunted trails through spectral nights,
Ghostly steps on ancient stones.
Guiding through the dream-filled flights,
Where the midnight spirit roams.

Hallowed Paths

Sacred walk through hallowed ground,
Where the air with reverence sings.
Timeless echoes all around,
Speak of ageless, hidden things.

Whispers from the past abide,
In the shadows of the trees.
Guiding souls with gentle stride,
Through the path where mystics breeze.

Journeys end and new begin,
On the trail of life's embrace.
Sacred steps in whispered hymn,
Find their peace in holy grace.

Galactic Paths

Wander soft through cosmic night,
Stars aglow in misty flight.
Nebulae paint trails so vast,
On galactic paths we cast.

Planets orbit, silent spheres,
Echoes whisper ancient years.
Comets blaze with tails of fire,
In this endless, star-knit choir.

Dark and light in balance play,
Distant galaxies in sway.
Celestial shadows gently drift,
Bearing secrets, timeless gift.

Ethereal Drifts

Through the void, a spectral dance,
Stars and shadows in a trance.
Whispers of the cosmic wind,
On ethereal drifts, we spin.

Veils of light in silence part,
Tracing lines of stellar art.
Galaxies in dreams unfold,
Tales of wonder yet untold.

Celestial ships in twilight glide,
Through the boundless, starry tide.
Mystic realms of space we sift,
Lost in endless, ethereal drift.

Moon's Radiance Road

Beneath the gleaming twilight show,
Soft whispers arise from the shadows.
A path is lit by lunar beams,
Guiding dreams and silent streams.

Stars adorn the velvet sky,
Where wishes travel, spirits fly.
The road of light and wonder leads,
To realms of magic, hearts freed.

Mysteries unfold in silver hues,
In night, where dreams fuse.
Steps echo in the tranquil night,
Led by moon's soft, gentle light.

Through the forest, ancient, grand,
Footprints dance upon the sand.
A voyage embraced by night,
Endless, serene, pure delight.

Moonlit Wanderings

In the hush of twilight's glow,
Whispers of night begin to flow.
Softly treading paths unseen,
In the realm of moonlit sheen.

Shadows play and softly blend,
With dreams, where hearts befriend.
Steps take journeys far and wide,
In the light, where spirits bide.

Glimmers dance on leaf and bough,
Illuminating the silent vow.
To traverse this serene, bright land,
Guided by night's gentle hand.

Horizon kissed by silver's touch,
Mysteries held within its clutch.
Each step in enchanted maze,
Unfolds the night's wondrous phase.

Silhouetted Routes

Shapes of dusk and shadows sway,
Marking paths where dreams lay.
Moon's embrace wraps the night,
Guiding ways in soft, pale light.

Whispers echo through the trees,
With every hush, a gentle breeze.
Steps of silence through the night,
Where shadows dance in gentle flight.

Forests deep and valleys low,
Bathe in moonlight's gentle glow.
Turns and bends in shaded paths,
Follow trails of midnight drafts.

Night's grace upon the ground,
Footsteps lead, without a sound.
Through the veil of twilight's kiss,
Journey into realms of bliss.

Glowing Path Trails

A lane beset by moon's soft gleam,
Where hopes and dreams together teem.
Through the night, a path unfolds,
Guided by the light it holds.

Bare feet touch the glowing lane,
In moonlight's song, free of chains.
Step by step, a tale unwinds,
Of secret paths and hidden signs.

Silent echoes in the leaves,
Tell of stories no one grieves.
The trail of light so pure, so bold,
Casts aside the dark and cold.

Wanderers in search of peace,
Follow trails where shadows cease.
In the glow of twilight's veil,
Find the night's enchanting tale.

Gleaming Avenues

Beneath the urban sky so vast,
Lights shimmer, reflections cast.
Ancient avenues gleam and glow,
In a dance of time's constant flow.

Whispers of stories old and new,
Merge within the city's hue.
Echoes of laughter, shades of tears,
Painted lanes of dreams and fears.

Cobblestones and pathways bright,
Twist and turn in evening light.
Mysteries wrapped in pavement cold,
Silent secrets, truths untold.

Wandering souls in ceaseless roam,
Find the streets a second home.
Every step on hallowed ground,
In silent rhythms, hearts are bound.

Cosmic Passageways

Through the vast and silent night,
Planets drift in quiet flight.
Galaxies in whispered tune,
Dance beneath the silver moon.

Nebulas in colors grand,
Stretch across the star-filled sand.
Pathways carved in stardust trails,
Lead to where the light prevails.

Comets blaze in fleeting grace,
Marking time and endless space.
Ever onward, tails unfurled,
Tracing lines across the world.

A sea of stars, a cosmic wave,
Holds the secrets that we crave.
Infinite, the roads unfold,
Stories of the universe told.

Shadows and Glows

In the twilight's mellow gleam,
Contrasts dance in silent dream.
Shadows, glows in soft embrace,
Weave a tapestry of grace.

Lantern light in evening dusk,
Warms the air with amber musk.
Silhouettes in fleeting view,
Draw the night in shades of blue.

Whispers of the day retreat,
Dark and light in harmonious beat.
Glowing embers, fading sighs,
Whisper secrets of the skies.

Through the night, the story flows,
Of this dance of shadows, glows.
Mingling in a silent song,
Night and light where dreams belong.

Velvet Skyways

On the velvet paths of night,
Stars are dots in endless flight.
Wings of dreams in cosmic streams,
Fly beyond our wildest schemes.

Moonbeams cast a gentle lace,
Softly cradling the sky's face.
Through this cloak of deepest blue,
Mysteries of the night ensue.

Whispers in the starlit breeze,
Carry hopes across the seas.
Velvet skyways, vast and grand,
Hold us in their tender hand.

Silent is the midnight air,
Cloaked in magic, pure and rare.
Every twinkle, every glow,
Guides the heart to realms below.

Twilight Tracks

Beneath the amethyst sky, we cross the silent lane,
Whispers of moonlight dance in soft refrain.
Twilight kisses the earth with gentle grace,
Leaving silver trails on our lonely pace.

Shadows stretch, embracing our quiet path,
Stars awaken, escaping daylight's wrath.
Each footfall sings a melody so sweet,
Echoes of dusk where two worlds meet.

Lanterns of fireflies flicker in the mist,
Their light entwined in night's tender twist.
Hearts beat with the rhythm of the dark,
Guided by the faintest celestial spark.

The skyline melts into shades of deep blue,
As twilight waltzes, bidding day adieu.
And on these twilight tracks we tread,
Meeting dreams where angels fear to tread.

Silverlit Journeys

Underneath the silver sky's embrace,
Our hearts entwine in a timeless space.
Footprints marked in a moonlit trance,
We wander free in our cosmic dance.

The whispering wind carries tales of old,
Stories of love that remain untold.
Through valleys bright with lunar beams,
We chase the shadows of our dreams.

Stars above, in their endless flight,
Guide our spirits through the night.
With every step, our souls ignite,
Wrapped in the cloak of celestial light.

Mystic paths we've yet to stride,
On silverlit journeys side by side.
Eternity unfolds in each midnight hour,
Our hearts like flowers in the starlight shower.

Eclipsed Passages

In the quiet of an eclipse's hold,
Ancient secrets quietly unfold.
Shadows dance on the passageway,
Whispering stories of yesterday.

The moon's soft veil covers the night,
Drawing dreams in pale twilight.
Eclipsed passages of time reveal,
Mysteries the stars conceal.

Walking through this twilight maze,
We lose ourselves in a phantom haze.
Every step a ballet in the dark,
Imprinted by an ethereal mark.

Ghostly trails under lunar gaze,
A fleeting touch in a timeless phase.
On these eclipsed paths we glide,
Finding solace in where we hide.

Nocturnal Routes

Through the fabric of night we weave,
On paths only dreams perceive.
Nocturnal routes bathed in lunar glow,
Leading us where few dare to go.

With whispers of the wind as our guide,
We journey on, side by side.
The stars above, a celestial dome,
Marking the trails that call us home.

Silence sings the songs of old,
In voices soft, in tales bold.
We wander where the worlds subside,
In the still of night, where secrets hide.

Each shadow casts its gentle trace,
In the midnight's tender embrace.
On nocturnal routes we travel far,
Guided by the light of a distant star.

Galactic Trips

Beyond the stars, where dreams take flight,
In the silence of the endless night,
Galactic winds guide our ship,
On boundless, cosmic summer trips.

Nebulae bloom like flowers fair,
And comet's tails streak the air,
In orbits vast, we drift and sway,
Through the Milky Way's grand ballet.

Planets spin in colors bold,
Stories of space-time they unfold,
From black holes to the edge of space,
We journey on in this vast embrace.

Constellations paint the sky,
Winking an astral lullaby,
Voyaging where galaxies collide,
Swirling in an infinite tide.

With stardust in our travelers' wake,
New worlds our eager hearts do make,
On galactic trips where dreams take flight,
Exploring the universe, depths, and heights.

Moonbridge Adventures

A silver arc in twilight's glow,
Moonbridge leads where dreams do flow,
Mystic paths of lunar light,
In twilight's heart, we'll take our flight.

Crater lakes with sapphire gleam,
Reflect the cosmos, like a dream,
Through moon-soaked lands, our spirits roam,
Finding ancient paths to call our own.

With every step, new wonders rise,
Woven threads of cosmic ties,
Echoes of the past resound,
In lunar silence, all around.

Mountains tall, in shadows deep,
Secrets of the ages keep,
On this bridge of endless seas,
Adventures in moonlight's breeze.

We'll journey 'neath the silver dome,
Amongst the stars, we'll find our home,
On Moonbridge trails, where dreams are spun,
Adventures sparkled by the moon's own sun.

Celestial Quests

Above the skies, where dreams ignite,
We rise on wings of pure delight,
Celestial quests, for hearts so bold,
Exploring tales the cosmos told.

Through star-kissed realms and nebulae,
Our journey finds new skies to sway,
In meteor rain, with trails afire,
We chase our ever-rising desire.

Galaxies whirl in vibrant dance,
A symphony of pure expanse,
In every twinkle, a story's cast,
In celestial wanderings so vast.

We chart the stars, our path unseen,
In the universe, we chase the sheen,
Beyond the fabric of space and time,
Bound by the endless, cosmic rhyme.

In questing hearts, dreams intertwine,
With stardust on our steps, divine,
Celestial quests, where souls align,
Embracing the beauty of the infinite line.

Moon-Kissed Roads

Where shadows lie and stars do peek,
On moon-kissed roads, our hearts we seek,
In twilight's hush, where whispers play,
We wander 'neath the Milky Way.

With silver beams upon our trail,
Through valleys deep and misty veil,
In lunar glow, a path unfolds,
Mysteries of the night it holds.

Craters carved by time's own hand,
In silent grace, these markings stand,
On moon-kissed roads of ancient lore,
We journey far, we dream once more.

Stars above in endless sprawl,
Guide us through the celestial hall,
Each footstep light with echoes past,
On roads where time and space contrast.

Embraced by night's gentle embrace,
We find ourselves in this vast space,
On moon-kissed roads where dreams are told,
In silver light, hearts pure and bold.

Lunar Labyrinth

In the maze of midnight's glow,
Silver paths and shadows flow,
Whispered secrets softly creep,
Stars above in silence weep.

Mystic routes of ancient lore,
Tracing tales of times before,
Moonlit streams in twilight's thrall,
Echoes of the nightfall call.

Hidden dreams and phantom sights,
Dance in beams of opal light,
Curves and turns of lunar lace,
Leading on in endless chase.

Wisps of wonder, whispers pale,
Through the labyrinth, we sail,
Night unfolds its silken threads,
Guiding weary, wandering heads.

Endless paths and mirrored dreams,
Twisting through the starlit seams,
Lunar light our guide, our friend,
Till the labyrinth finds its end.

Starlit Trails

Paths alight in cosmic glow,
Where the astral breezes blow,
In the heavens' vast expanse,
Stars invite us to their dance.

Glimmering trails through velvet night,
Leading dreams in silent flight,
Constellations pave the way,
Guardians till the break of day.

Whispers of the ancient skies,
Tales unfold where stardust lies,
Walking through celestial haze,
In the starlit trails we gaze.

Serenade of twilight's song,
Guided by the stars along,
Journey through the endless sphere,
Hearts alight, we have no fear.

Glistening paths of silver threads,
Weaving through where cosmos spreads,
Starlit trails our guiding beams,
Lighting up our twilight dreams.

Moonbeam Mazes

Glistening webs of silver light,
Weave a maze within the night,
Through the shadows, paths do wind,
Secrets hidden, hard to find.

Silent whispers call us forth,
Guiding south and leading north,
Moonbeams form the twisted ways,
Leading on through night's embrace.

Softly tread on lunar gold,
Mysteries of night unfold,
Each new turn a tale untold,
In the maze, the dreams are bold.

Veils of light and shadows play,
In this maze, we often stray,
Yet the night with gentle grace,
Guides us through the moonbeam's maze.

Silken threads of lunar beams,
Crafting paths from hidden dreams,
In the maze, we lose our time,
Moonlit paths our hearts align.

Celestial Corridors

Hallways lit by cosmic glow,
Through the skies the pathways flow,
Celestial lights our guide and friend,
Endless corridors transcend.

Vaulted skies of midnight blue,
Stars above in silver hue,
Walk the paths of light and shade,
In these corridors we're laid.

Dreams and wonders waiting still,
Mortal minds they gently fill,
Nebulae like hidden doors,
Opening to magic shores.

Silent steps on starlit floor,
Every turn reveals much more,
Celestial corridors us steer,
Through the night, sincere and clear.

Eternal paths of ancient lore,
Stretching far through night and more,
In these corridors we find,
Echoes of the cosmic mind.

Milky Way Tracks

In the night the stars align,
Forming pathways oh so fine.
Celestial rivers in the dark,
Guiding dreams with a spark.

Cosmic dust in gentle flow,
On this journey, we all go.
Galaxies whisper sweet refrains,
Through the vast, endless plains.

Nebulas glow a gentle hue,
Under skies so deep and blue.
Planets spin in rhythmic trance,
In this timeless cosmic dance.

Constellations mark the way,
To dawn of a brand new day.
Each star a story, each light a guide,
As we drift on this astral tide.

Milky Way, your tracks we trace,
In this boundless, open space.
Wonder fills our hearts this night,
In your glow, our spirits take flight.

Moonlit Meanderings

Silver beams on cobblestone,
Casting shadows all alone.
Whispers from the moonlit breeze,
Through the night, they gently tease.

Footsteps echo soft and light,
Guided by the soft moonlight.
Silent paths through old port towns,
'Neath the sky, in velvet gowns.

Lanterns flicker in the night,
With a warm and gentle light.
Stories from a bygone age,
On the streets, their ghosts engage.

Softly glows the lunar face,
Bathing all in tender grace.
Wanderers in the quiet night,
Finding peace in gentle light.

Moonlit meanderings we take,
While the world begins to wake.
In the stillness of the night,
Hearts find solace, pure delight.

Twilight Avenue

Dusky hues on twilight's lane,
Gentle whispers, night's refrain.
Birds sing soft a lullaby,
As the sun bids day goodbye.

Lights flicker in shadowed streets,
Where the evening peace competes.
With the songs of stars so bright,
Twinkling softly in the night.

Trees cast long and shadowed forms,
In the cool of evening warms.
Silhouettes dance in the breeze,
Like gentle whispers through the trees.

Evening's cloak of purple deep,
Holds the world in tender keep.
Each step down this avenue,
Steals a heartbeat, one or two.

As the sky fades into night,
Twilight's glow a fading light.
Memories on this path, renewed,
Down the tranquil, twilight avenue.

Celestial Adventures

Galactic winds and solar gales,
Through the cosmos, charting trails.
Stars like beacons guide our way,
In the night we find our stay.

Planets orbit, dance the skies,
Like a grand cosmic surprise.
Comets blaze their fiery mark,
Lighting up the endless dark.

Black holes whisper mysteries,
In the void, no boundaries.
Nebulas with colors blend,
Tales of space that never end.

Spaceships glide through ether bright,
Seeking out new stars in flight.
In this vast and wondrous sphere,
Every turn brings new frontier.

Celestial adventures call,
In this universe so tall.
With each star, our spirits soar,
In the quest for evermore.

Glistening Ways

In morning dew, the sunlight plays,
Reflecting beams in myriad rays
Upon the path where dreams alight,
Glistening ways in golden light.

Each step we take, with hope and glee,
Through forests deep or by the sea,
The journey's thread through night and day,
Is spun with love on glistening ways.

Beneath the boughs where shadows sway,
We find our course and there we stay,
The gentle breeze that softly lays,
Our weary hearts on glistening ways.

And when the stars begin to blaze,
We follow still those guiding rays,
With every breath, the heart obeys,
The endless call of glistening ways.

Moon-shadowed Routes

Through whispering woods where shadows meet,
The moonlight casts a path so sweet,
On ancient trails where silence flutes,
We wander down moon-shadowed routes.

Each turn reveals a different song,
Where lights and shadows dance along,
In silver beams, the heart confutes,
The mystery of moon-shadowed routes.

Through valleys deep and mountains tall,
The lunar light enchants us all,
With every step, the night refutes
The secrets of moon-shadowed routes.

In twilight's hue, where dreams concor,
We glide through realms we once implored,
The ink of night so keenly suits,
Our voyage on moon-shadowed routes.

Astral Alleyways

In realms where starlight weaves its threads,
Beyond the dreams of sleepy heads,
Lie paths of light through night displays,
We travel down the astral alleyways.

Each twinkling star, a guiding spark,
A beacon bright within the dark,
Through cosmic seas where silence stays,
We wander through the astral alleyways.

With every gleam, new worlds we see,
Infinite skies, a tapestry,
Connecting hearts with love's arrays,
Adrift along the astral alleyways.

And when the dawn begins to break,
We whisper farewell for our sake,
Yet in our hearts, forever stays,
The memory of astral alleyways.

Midnight Travels

When clocks strike twelve and night unfurls,
A hidden world of dreams uncurls,
In stillness deep, where silence revels,
We commence our midnight travels.

Through moonlit fields and shadowed glades,
The night reveals its soft cascades,
Of memories and tales the heart huddles,
In the trance of midnight travels.

With every step, the night's embrace,
Transforms the world to mystic place,
The compass guiding through the marvels,
Of starlit paths in midnight travels.

And as the dawn begins to crest,
We find within our hearts a rest,
A peace that only night unravels,
The magic of our midnight travels.

Evening's Glow Paths

Hues of amber bathe the ground,
Whispers of twilight do abound,
Softly tread where shadows play,
In the fading light of day.

Crickets chirp their evening song,
As the night begins to throng,
Gentle breezes kiss the air,
In a dance of sheer affair.

Golden glimmers through the trees,
Rustling leaves in twilight's breeze,
Paths beneath the evening's glow,
Guide the wanderers who know.

Stars begin their whispered chime,
Marking space and gifting time,
Moonlight cast in silver streams,
Painting pathways with their dreams.

Softly tread where shadows play,
In the fading light of day,
Golden glimmers through the trees,
Rustling leaves in twilight's breeze.

Radiant Voyageways

Sunset paints the sky with grace,
Embers of the day's embrace,
Voyageways lit by twilight's hand,
Guide the hearts upon this land.

Ocean waves reflect the hues,
Of a sky in red and blues,
Journey forth on evening's tide,
With the stars as gentle guide.

Radiance in each step we take,
Footsteps form as dreams awake,
Drifting on the twilight's breeze,
Wandering where hearts can ease.

Lanterns light the cobbled path,
Glimmers shine in evening's bath,
Voyageways beneath the sky,
With the stars to light the high.

Voyageways lit by twilight's hand,
Guide the hearts upon this land,
Radiance in each step we take,
Footsteps form as dreams awake.

Night-Dappled Trails

Whispers of the forest speak,
Through the night, the moonlight sleek,
Dappled trails that twist and sway,
Carried by the stars' array.

Owls call among the trees,
Echoed through the midnight breeze,
Mystic paths where shadows roam,
Guiding souls to find their home.

Underneath the canopy,
Night's embrace as deep as sea,
Wandering the trails tonight,
In the glow of silver light.

Fireflies create their dance,
In a symphony of chance,
Paths of shadows, paths of light,
Guiding through the velvet night.

Dappled trails that twist and sway,
Carried by the stars' array,
Underneath the canopy,
Night's embrace as deep as sea.

Silvery Walkways

Moonlit paths of silver glow,
Guiding footsteps, soft and slow,
Walkways kissed by lunar beams,
Whispering the night's sweet dreams.

Silent realms beneath the sky,
Where the stars in stillness lie,
Paths of dust and ancient lore,
Lead to places known before.

Winding trails that shimmer bright,
Underneath the soft moonlight,
Every stone a piece of art,
Etched within the wanderer's heart.

Echoes of the midnight call,
Dancing shadows, standing tall,
Walkways of a silvery hue,
Show the journey brave and true.

Guiding footsteps, soft and slow,
Paths of dust and ancient lore,
Winding trails that shimmer bright,
Every stone a piece of art.

Moonlight Marmalade

In jars where moonbeams softly lay,
We spread the stars with each new day,
A silver glaze on dreams begun,
As night yields gently to the sun.

The night's embrace, a velvet spread,
With whispers of what stars have said,
On toast of time, we savor more,
In moonlight's jar, though gone before.

Sweet marmalade of lunar light,
We taste the echoes of the night,
Preserved in jars of cosmic glow,
A dance in light as shadows grow.

In every spoonful, night prevails,
With stories wrapped in moonlit tales,
We spread the dreams on morning's bread,
And savor what the moon has fed.

Nocturnal Escapades

In realms where nighttime shadows play,
Adventures in the dark hold sway,
Beyond the stars where dreams explore,
The mysteries of the night implore.

We sail through skies on whisper's breeze,
With moonlit winds and starlit seas,
Nocturnal paths we dare to tread,
In secret worlds inside our head.

Each twilight brings a hidden quest,
Where hearts of night find no rest,
We chase the comets, wild and free,
Through galaxies of fantasy.

Beneath the veil of silent skies,
Nocturnal dreams materialize,
In every whisper, every shade,
Our souls embark, unafraid.

Glistening Voyages

The starry charts of midnight sea,
Map constellations wild and free,
With sails of light and anchors thin,
Our glistening voyages begin.

Through cosmic tides and lunar streams,
Our vessel flows on waves of dreams,
Nebulae guide our silent way,
Lit by the echoes of the day.

In twilight's port of velvet black,
We'll dock and leave but turn not back,
For every journey yet untold,
Is cast in hues of silver and gold.

In cosmic harbors deep and wide,
We drift on stardust, side by side,
To sail the night and find new shores,
Where glistening wonders wait in stores.

Twilight Wanderings

When twilight casts its purple veil,
And starlight whispers soft as tale,
We wander through the dusk's embrace,
In silent steps, we find our place.

Through meadows where the shadows sleep,
The mysteries of twilight keep,
Each step a dance with dusk and dawn,
In twilight's glow, our spirits drawn.

By rivers made of evening's hue,
With skies of indigo and blue,
We wander on, free and unbound,
In twilight's realm where souls are found.

Each twilight dusk, a world reborn,
Of dreams and wonders to adorn,
We walk the line 'twixt night and day,
In twilight wanderings, we stay.

Astral Excursions

Through stars we pierce the night
In whispers soft, alight
Galaxies unfold, in sight
An endless cosmic flight

Comets blaze a fiery trail
Nebulae in colors pale
Planets dance in rhythm frail
In cosmos grand, we sail

Across the void, vast and clear
Silent echoes we adhere
Mysteries to us draw near
Without a hint of fear

Celestial winds with grace
Guide us through the starry space
Infinite, this timeless chase
In the universe's embrace

With wonder, hearts ignite
In realms of ethereal light
Astral dreams take flight
Beyond the mere mortal night

Night's Glimmering Roads

Underneath the twilight skies
Glimmers where the darkness lies
Footprints trace where silence cries
On paths where the old moon flies

Wisps of light and shadows blend
In corridors that have no end
Mystic ways that gently bend
As night and dream suspend

Stars are lanterns on our quest
Guiding to the unknown best
In the night, we find our rest
Each step a whispered test

Echoes of the ancient lore
Resonate forevermore
Through roads that midnight bore
From dreams to waking's shore

In night's embrace, we've roved
On glimmering roads, we've loved
Through stellar darks, we've dove
With the heavens speaking of

Moonshine Walks

Beneath the pale moonlight
We walk in dreams so bright
Shadows soften, take flight
In the magic of the night

Silvery beams in streams
Illuminate our dreams
Whispering in gentle themes
Of celestial, soft gleams

The world in quiet sway
Under lunar rays' play
In night's tender array
We wander, gently stray

Hand in hand, we find
Peace with an open mind
In moonlit paths, entwined
Dreams and fates aligned

In moonshine's tender glow
Through tranquil paths we go
Below the night's calm flow
Hearts in starlight, slow

Evening Rays Route

As sunset paints the skies
In gold and crimson dyes
We walk where daylight dies
And evening softly sighs

The hues of twilight blend
In time that seems to bend
Until the day's bright end
And stars begin to send

Whispers of the night
In breezes soft, so light
Guide us through day's twilight
To the deep and quiet night

On paths of fading sun
Where twilight has begun
In evening's gentle run
Dreams and reality are one

With each step, the light recedes
Night's calmness intercedes
On evening rays, our needs
To dawning stars, it leads

Shimmering Roads

Beneath the sun's warm golden touch,
The roads do gleam with subtle light.
With every step, a gentle hush,
As day transforms into the night.

Mirage of dreams, where shadows play,
In incandescent, winding lanes,
And every footfall weaves its way,
Through whispered tales of joy and pains.

Stars above do softly guide,
Their shimmer bright, a cosmic thread,
A path where hearts in silence bide,
And follow dreams yet left unsaid.

The world, it hums a quiet tune,
Through forests green and deserts wide,
Each road a chance to chase the moon,
And let the wind of fate decide.

In twilight's glow, we find our peace,
On roads that shimmer, gently sway,
A journey's end that brings release,
And promises of a new day.

Enchanted Expeditions

Through forests dense, where shadows dance,
The air is thick with magic's song.
Each step a stride in mystic trance,
Through realms where faeries do belong.

Mountains rise with ancient might,
Their peaks adorned in silver veils.
Every path, a new delight,
Where whispered winds tell timeless tales.

Oceans vast, with waves that gleam,
Reflect the skies, so deep and wide.
An endless blue, a sailor's dream,
Where mermaids in the waters hide.

Tempest skies and rainbow hue,
Paint the world in colors bold.
Expeditions brave and true,
Where secrets of the wild unfold.

Every dawn, a fresh surprise,
Enchantment woven through each sight.
On these journeys under skies,
We chase the magic of the night.

Ethereal Excursions

In realms between the day and night,
Where dreams and waking life converge,
We wander paths of mystic light,
In echoes where our souls emerge.

Celestial whispers, soft and clear,
Guide us through this spectral plane.
In every heartbeat, visions near,
As stars above begin their reign.

Mists that curl like ancient lore,
Envelop us in tender grace.
Each footfall on this phantom floor,
Unravels time and space's trace.

Through veils of twilight, shadows blend,
With hues of dusk and dawn's embrace,
In worlds where spirits gently tend,
An endless dance, a timeless chase.

Ethereal wings, in silent flight,
Lead us through the boundless skies.
Excursions where the night grows bright,
In endless realms where wonder lies.

Serene Byways

In quiet lanes where silence sings,
The byways wind through fields of green.
A gentle breeze on feathered wings,
Invites a pause in the serene.

Each step along the time-worn path,
Reveals a story softly told.
The whispers of the aftermath,
In moments brushed with flecks of gold.

The rivers hum a tender tune,
Their waters calm, a soothing flow.
Reflecting soft the sky's maroon,
As twilight sets the world aglow.

Through forests deep, where shadows play,
And sunlight filters through the leaves,
We wander on, both night and day,
In peace the heart of nature weaves.

Beneath the stars, a quiet vow,
In stillness, find the soul's repose.
On byways blessed, the world allows,
A gentle space where beauty grows.

Celestial Boulevards

Under a sky of midnight blue,
Twinkling lights lead the way,
On boulevards of stars so true,
In the vast cosmic array.

Galaxies spill like glittering streams,
Across an infinite night,
Wandering souls share dreams,
Illuminated by starlight.

Nebulae paint the horizon wide,
With hues of pink and gold,
On celestial boulevards we glide,
Stories of the universe unfold.

Silent whispers through the dark,
Guide us with gentle hand,
On paths where astral echoes spark,
In this expansive, boundless land.

Up in the heavens where we belong,
Among the stars and eternal night,
The celestial boulevards hum a song,
To the heart that seeks the light.

Starpath Reflections

Midnight's mirror reflects the sky,
Every star a shining face,
In the silence, dreams amplify,
A tranquil, infinite space.

The path of light, a river pure,
Guiding footsteps one by one,
Each twinkle a beacon to ensure,
The journey to a distant sun.

Footprints on this starry lane,
Echo softly from ages past,
Through cosmos by fate ordained,
Questions eternal everlast.

Radiant beams whisper low,
Tales of cosmos, ever bright,
On starpaths where reflections flow,
In the gentle grip of night.

From nebulous clouds to galaxies far,
A dance of light that never ends,
Starpath reflections are who we are,
Eternal souls and cosmic friends.

Eclipsed Routes

Through the shadow's gentle veil,
Eclipsed routes lead us on,
By the moon's ethereal trail,
As night folds into dawn.

Celestial rhythms softly play,
A dance of light and dark,
On these paths where shadows sway,
Leaving an ephemeral mark.

Between the stars and moonlit beams,
We wander through the night,
In search of truth in silvery dreams,
Beneath an eclipsed light.

Mysteries of the shaded sky,
Whisper secrets, old yet wise,
On routes where shadows quietly fly,
Past the veil of earthly ties.

The eclipsed routes reveal the way,
To realms beyond our sight,
Guiding each step we bravely sway,
In the balance of dark and light.

Ethereal Pathways

In realms where dreams and stars align,
Ethereal pathways unfold,
Guided by a spark divine,
Through the cosmos, brave and bold.

We tread on light, soft and pure,
On pathways spun from stardust fine,
Each step taken seems so sure,
As planets and moons intertwine.

Nebulous whispers greet the dawn,
On paths where time stands still,
Towards horizons yet unborn,
Through space where hearts can fill.

Stellar winds our guide and friend,
Through pathways void of fear,
On routes that never truly end,
Where every answer seems so near.

Beneath the skies of endless night,
Ethereal pathways brightly shine,
Leading us with gentle light,
To the love that is divine.

Stellar Paths

Under the night, where stars align,
We wander through the ancient sign.
Whispers of cosmos, softly found,
Tracing paths where dreams abound.

Silent trails in twilight skies,
Galaxy's gaze in countless eyes.
Each step a story, each breath a wish,
A celestial dance in the starry swish.

Constellations paint our way,
Guiding hearts that gently sway.
In the realm where stardust lies,
Hope is born, and never dies.

Celestial road, with light so pure,
Eternal guide to dreams obscure.
Nebulae hum a gentle tune,
'Neath the glow of silver moon.

Promise kept in the night's embrace,
Stellar paths we shall trace.
A universe within our sight,
Wandering through endless night.

Glowing Crossings

Beneath the sky of endless hues,
Glow the crossings we must choose.
Paths that glisten, where shadows trace,
In the twilight's warm embrace.

Golden beams through darkened night,
Guiding souls with gentle light.
Guardian stars, our way they show,
Leading hearts where dreams may flow.

Through the veil of evening's breath,
We traverse the stars above our death.
Each crossing a new world's gate,
Interwoven strands of fate.

Infinite journeys on stardust lanes,
Where the glow of heart remains.
A soul's passage, bright and clear,
Through the crossings, without fear.

Ever there, where dreams collide,
In the universe, vast and wide.
Glowing crossings, alight with cheer,
Illuminate our hearts so dear.

Astral Alleys

In the alleys of the vast and deep,
Where cosmic secrets quiet sleep.
Wanderers tread on wisps of light,
Questing hearts in the velvet night.

Nebula's glow in shrouded lanes,
Mysteries in endless chains.
Each step reveals a silent song,
In the alleys where we belong.

Twinkling paths that softly bend,
Guiding lights that never end.
Through astral alleys, dreams take flight,
Boundless wonder in the night.

Galactic tales in quiet ways,
Etched in the stars' eternal gaze.
Hidden nooks of cosmic lore,
Astral alleys, evermore.

Every turn a new embrace,
Infinite in time and space.
Astral alleys, surreal and grand,
Hold the secrets of this land.

Dream-lit Directions

In the hush of midnight's breath,
Dream-lit paths defy all death.
Glowing trails of spectral beams,
Guide our hearts through endless dreams.

Shadows dance in quiet night,
Whispers cradle dreams so bright.
Mystic guides in realms unseen,
Points of light where souls convene.

Through the night's ethereal scheme,
Follow dreams like flowing stream.
Every star a guidepost fair,
Woven through the midnight air.

Boundless skies in twilight's grace,
In the stars our hopes we trace.
Dream-lit paths in cosmic tides,
To the soul's true home it guides.

Infinite directions lead,
Where the stars and dreams proceed.
Dream-lit journeys, soft and clear,
Carry hearts both far and near.

Midnight Roads

Whispering winds through night's embrace,
Lonely streets without a trace.
Sojourner's steps, a silent dance,
Beneath the moon's entrancing glance.

Lamp posts glow with amber light,
Guiding hearts in darkest night.
Shadows drift in soft parade,
Dreams and memories start to fade.

Oceans vast, a city's hum,
Midnight roads where spirits come.
Whistle of the twilight breeze,
Whispers tales among the trees.

Twinkling stars in heaven's dome,
Wandering souls find their home.
Lost in time, the night unfolds,
Secrets shared, and stories told.

Silent echoes, paths unknown,
Midnight roads by moonlight shown.
Every step, a journey made,
Every heart, a masquerade.

Polaris Journeys

Guiding light, the northern star,
Beckons travelers from afar.
Polaris glows in midnight skies,
Leading souls where destiny lies.

Wanderers on timeless quests,
Seek the truth that never rests.
Beneath the sky's celestial tides,
Hearts and thoughts the star confides.

Cold winds whisper secrets old,
Tales of brave and hearts of gold.
Journeys chased by fearless few,
Underneath the starlight's view.

Eternal beacon, never lost,
Through unknowns we pay the cost.
Polaris stands to light the way,
Through night until the break of day.

With every step, the path untold,
Marking dreams both brave and bold.
Journey forth with light in hand,
Guided by Polaris's command.

Lunar Footsteps

Moonlit paths of silver hue,
Silent echoes calling you.
Tread the steps of ancient lore,
Where legends walked in times before.

Gentle glow of lunar beams,
Weaving through our midnight dreams.
Each footfall sounds a whispered note,
Upon the night's soft velvet coat.

Shadow dances, waltz of light,
Steps that traverse through the night.
Guided by the moon's embrace,
In this calm and quiet space.

Eons past, yet ever new,
Lunar paths where wishes grew.
Truth and wonder softly blend,
As we journey to the end.

Every footprint tells a tale,
Moonlit stories, soft and frail.
Step by step, we find our way,
Underneath the night's display.

Starlit Travels

Starlit paths through endless skies,
Where dreams and cosmos softly rise.
Traveler's heart in twilight's keep,
Wanders where the angels weep.

Galaxies in velvet spread,
Whisper tales of stars long dead.
Cosmic winds and comet trails,
Guide our paths where courage sails.

Eyes alight with astral gleam,
Following the midnight dream.
Stardust whispers in the breeze,
Filling nights with tales and ease.

Journey far and travel wide,
On the waves of space and tide.
Every star a friend and guide,
On this starlit cosmic ride.

Infinity above unfolds,
Starlit travels, tales untold.
Through the night, the heart explores,
All the magic starlight stores.

Shining Trails

In the forest, shadows wane,
Whispers echo, soft refrains,
Leaves dance on a gentle breeze,
Nature hums, her sweet decease.

Golden threads weave through the night,
Stars bestow their ancient light,
Owls call out their nightly quest,
In the dark, the heart finds rest.

Silence breathes a solemn tune,
Guidance from the silver moon,
Paths of gold beneath our feet,
Echoes of a world replete.

Crickets sing their twilight song,
Hours drift, the night is long,
Footsteps traced in stardust soil,
Dreams unfurl, their subtle coil.

Mysteries in night's embrace,
Find their home in quiet grace,
Twinkling lights to forge our way,
Through the dark until the day.

Lunar Journeys

Beneath the sky, in midnight's veil,
Stories of old begin to sail,
Moonlight bathes the earthly sphere,
Casting spells so crystal clear.

Whispers glide on silken air,
Echoes of a time so rare,
Dreams take wing on life's grand stage,
Written on the lunar page.

Silver beams through treetops weave,
Memories of dusk reprieve,
Journeys start with gentle steps,
Within the heart, the secret kept.

Stars align, their paths entwined,
Guiding lights for hearts confined,
Silent night and tranquil seas,
Draw the soul towards its peace.

Echoes of the past collide,
With the present, side by side,
Lunar journeys vast and grand,
Traveling through this mystic land.

Moonlit Trails

In the cloak of night unfurled,
Mysteries of a forgotten world,
Steps traced by the pale moon's glow,
Whisper secrets only we know.

Soft light filters through the trees,
Dances with the evening breeze,
Leaves rustle in a hushed affair,
Nature's breath, a silent prayer.

Winding paths of silver dust,
Guiding through the night we trust,
Each step, a story left untold,
In moonlit trails, our dreams unfold.

Soft hoots of an owl nearby,
Underneath the starlit sky,
Silent shadows come and pass,
Marking trails upon the grass.

Journeys made in gentle grace,
Followed by night's warm embrace,
In moonlit trails, our souls unite,
Guided by the tranquil night.

Nocturnal Passages

In the hush of deep twilight,
Nocturnal wings take flight,
Owls whisper wisdom, soft and low,
In realms where moonbeams flow.

Silent streams reflect the stars,
Guiding travelers from afar,
Nature's choir begins to sing,
Soft, as midnight secrets bring.

Lunar rivers through the dark,
Guide our souls with ethereal spark,
Steps unseen in spectral mist,
On paths unknown, by shadows kissed.

Beneath the arch of night's domain,
Dreamers wander through the plain,
Lit by ancient lunar glow,
In quiet reverie, they go.

Nocturnal passages unfold,
Woven tales in silence told,
Guided by the stars so bright,
Through the long and gentle night.

Aurora Alleys

Through alleys of aurora dreams,
In twilight's glowing, silent seams,
We wander where the night sky beams,
And trace the constellations' schemes.

Neon whispers, colors blend,
Skyward paths that twist and bend,
Follow now, the hues transcend,
To where the cosmic realms extend.

A dance of lights, a spectral show,
Guide us where the shadows grow,
Into the night, where stardust flows,
Beneath the skies, our spirits glow.

In alleyways of northern light,
We sail on splendored wings of night,
Lost in wonder, pure delight,
In endless hues of emerald bright.

Cascading from the heavens' veil,
Auroras weave their mystic trail,
Eerie shades that gently hail,
In cosmic reverie, we sail.

Moonlit Voyages

Upon the sea, with moon as guide,
We set our sails, the tides we ride,
Beneath the night, with stars our side,
In whispered winds, our hearts confide.

A silver path falls 'cross the wave,
By moonlight's glow, so soft and brave,
Through mist and lore, the seas behave,
In quiet calm, our souls we save.

Each cresting wave, a lullaby,
The ocean's breath, a gentle sigh,
With moon above, our spirits fly,
Through endless night, beneath the sky.

Mariner dreams, by lunar gleam,
Guide us on this twilight stream,
Adrift in echoes, soft and serene,
In moonlit waves, we dare to dream.

As dawn approaches, shadows flee,
The stars above dissolve to sea,
Our voyage ends with morning's plea,
Yet moonlit wonders always be.

Heavenly Haunts

Through haunted paths of heavens' smiles,
Where stars commune in secret aisles,
We wander realms untouched by miles,
In whispered breaths, the night's beguiles.

Celestial spirits cast their glow,
Upon the world, their secrets show,
In quiet shadows, we move slow,
Where ancient mysteries tend to sow.

A ghostly dance of starry grace,
Echoes in this timeless space,
With each step we trace their place,
In silent cries, our fears efface.

Haunted dreams of outer spheres,
Bring forth memories, long-held tears,
In night's embrace, our shadows sheer,
In cosmic arcs that turn to years.

We walk the paths of spectral light,
In endless corridors of night,
Through heavenly haunts, the spirits' flight,
In timeless dance, we find our sight.

Starry Strolls

Beneath the dome of endless night,
We stroll where stars ignite,
In patterns old, their tales recite,
And guide us with their gentle light.

Each shimmer tells of times long gone,
A twinkling pulse, a cosmic song,
We wander forth, the night is young,
In starry paths where dreams belong.

The velvet night caresses all,
With silver whispers, vast and small,
In stillness deep, away from thrall,
We heed the quiet, night's soft call.

Our footsteps weave amongst the stars,
Beyond the reach of earthly bars,
In twilight's echo, where nothing mars,
With glistening lights, beyond the czars.

In peace, we stroll these endless skies,
With every step, a new sunrise,
The stars above, celestial ties,
Guide us through dark, where dreams arise.

Dreamlight Odyssey

Under the stars, in a twilight's embrace,
Whispers of secrets, through time and space,
A journey begins where reality bends,
In dreamlight odyssey, where magic ascends.

Velvet skies painted with cosmic hues,
Paths of wonder where the heart renews,
A symphony of dreams guides each stride,
In realms unknown, where spirits reside.

Mystic rivers flow with stardust streams,
Illuminating nights with golden beams,
Voyage through shadows, past gates unseen,
Embark on quests where destinies convene.

Through winding corridors of silent song,
We traverse realms where we truly belong,
Each step a chapter in an endless book,
In dreamlight odyssey, just one deeper look.

Echoes of memories etched in the night,
We chase the dawn, seeking the sight,
Of realms beyond, where fantasies play,
In a dreamlight odyssey, we'll forever stay.

Shimmering Sojourns

In fields of gold, where dreams alight,
We wander paths bathed in silver light,
Shimmering sojourns under moon's soft glow,
Where whispers of stars in silence flow.

Beneath the heavens, in quiet grace,
Our hearts align in a timeless place,
Mirages dance on horizons far,
Guiding our souls to where wonders are.

Each footfall echoes in the crystal air,
Through valleys deep, where shadows dare,
A seamless journey as the night unfurls,
In shimmering sojourns of hidden pearls.

Through ancient forests, 'neath canopies grand,
We find our truths with each grain of sand,
Ephemeral moments in the twilight's bind,
Shimmering sojourns in the realm of mind.

At the edge of dawn, as night withdraws,
We capture dreams within nature's laws,
In shimmering sojourns, both vast and bright,
We chase the day with the morning light.

Mystical Roads

On mystical roads where shadows blend,
We trace our steps to an unknown end,
Through forests dark and valleys wide,
Mystical roads where secrets hide.

The whispered winds tell ancient tales,
In moonlit nights where wonder sails,
We walk on paths where legends wake,
On mystical roads, our fates we make.

Lost in the mists of enchanted time,
Each step a rhythm, a silent rhyme,
Guided by stars in celestial codes,
We wander deep mystical roads.

With every turn, new vistas seen,
In a world that lies between,
Realms of magic and old abodes,
We find our way on mystical roads.

Bound by stories yet untold,
Carved in lore from days of old,
On mystical roads, our spirit flows,
To realms where eternal mystery grows.

Moonlit Corridors

Beneath the stars in silvery gleam,
We walk through corridors of a dream,
Moonlit paths where silence sings,
In night's embrace, our spirit springs.

Shadows dance in a gentle breeze,
Along the corridors through ancient trees,
Soft whispers brush through the quiet air,
Moonlit trails where we find our care.

In luminescent glow, shadows fade,
Revealing secrets, dreams are made,
Moonlit corridors, paths so bright,
Guide us gently through the night.

Through marble halls and mystic gates,
With every step, our soul awaits,
The dawn of dreams in soft repose,
In moonlit corridors, life's essence flows.

We wander far, in night's embrace,
Finding solace in this tranquil place,
Moonlit corridors of endless lore,
We journey, seeking forevermore.

Shimmer Routes

In twilight's gentle weave, the paths ignite,
With whispers of the dusk, in fading light.
Shimmer routes of dreams, by night's embrace,
Through stardust realms, we find our place.

Echoes of the past in every gleam,
Candles of hope in the river's seam.
Luminous trails of thoughts that guide,
In shimmer's glow, we softly glide.

Soft murmurs of the night air's song,
Bound in the shimmer, where souls belong.
A dance of shadows, a waltz of beams,
Amongst the stars and woven dreams.

Beneath the silver weeping skies,
The shimmer routes, in moon's devise.
Pathways cross in silent blight,
Leading hearts through endless night.

In hushed reverie, as moments pass,
Through shimmer routes, on silvered grass.
Cosmic threads our spirits tie,
To realms unknown, where shadows lie.

Starsway Journeys

Through starsway's arch, we tread the night,
Skies adorned with luminescent light.
A tapestry of endless trails,
Beyond the realms, where stardust hails.

Galaxies in whispered tones,
Sing of distant astral homes.
Guided by the milky streams,
We sail upon our starlit dreams.

Constellations mark our path,
Through the void, the aftermath.
Of cosmic tales and ancient lore,
On starsway journeys evermore.

Each footstep leaves a glittered trace,
In the boundless, endless space.
Through nebulae of folded hues,
Our spirits soar with night's muse.

In the silence of the spheres,
We write our stories, sans our fears.
On starsway journeys, bold and bright,
We wander through eternal night.

Wanderers of Moonlit Ways

Beneath the crescent's gentle glow,
In moonlit ways, our spirits flow.
Through shadows cast by silver beams,
We wander on, within our dreams.

Soft footfalls on the lunar sand,
A nomad's quest through twilight's land.
Myth and magic, woven tight,
In the embrace of the night.

The trees whisper their silent lore,
As moonlit paths we explore.
Each bend reveals a hidden light,
Guiding us through midnight's height.

Stars above, a jeweled crown,
In moonlit ways, we slow down.
Listening to the earth's soft sighs,
Underneath the velvet skies.

In every step, a glimpse of soul,
In moonlit's grasp, we find our goal.
Wanderers of ancient grace,
Moonlit ways our sacred place.

Twilight Trails

As dusk descends and day departs,
Twilight trails touch softened hearts.
A tapestry of fading hues,
Spreads across the sky's soft blues.

Shadows lengthen, calm and deep,
Through twilight trails, our secrets keep.
Gentle whispers in the air,
Guide us through the twilight's care.

In the dim light's tender fold,
Twilight trails, stories told.
Of forgotten dreams and silent sighs,
Underneath the twilight skies.

Stars begin their nightward bloom,
Twilight trails through growing gloom.
Paths we tread in quiet grace,
Finding peace in twilight's space.

As the night begins to rise,
In twilight trails, our spirits lie.
With the promise of the day's end,
In twilight's arms, we find a friend.

Whispering Walkways

Beneath the trees, where shadows play,
Soft whispers guide our steps astray.
In dappled light, we find our way,
Through secret paths of yesterday.

Leaves murmur tales of ancient lore,
Footfalls light on forest floor.
A sylvan spell, forevermore,
Enchants us as we wander forth.

Glimmers of sun in emerald lace,
Nature's echoes fill the space.
In reverent awe, we slow our pace,
Heartbeats join this sacred place.

Songs of old, a quiet breeze,
Whispers dance among the trees.
In this realm, our spirits ease,
Lost in nature's gentle tease.

Steps forgotten, trails unseen,
In the hush, our souls convene.
In whispers soft, and twilight sheen,
We tread where echoes softly glean.

Glistening Routes

Morning dew on grassy lanes,
Diamonds glint in sunlit gains.
Through the mist, a path retains,
Treasures found in tranquil strains.

Rivers sparkle, catch the light,
Guiding us from dawn to night.
Pebbles glow in mirrored sight,
Journeying within delight.

Golden rays on winding trails,
Softly kiss the hills and vales.
Crystal clear through morning veils,
Stories told in nature's tales.

Streams of silver, bright and pure,
Mark the pathways we endure.
In their flow, our hearts secure,
Promises of journeys sure.

In the shimmer, steps unfold,
Guided by the light of old.
Glistening routes their secrets hold,
Journey's end in stories told.

Nebula Navigations

Among the stars where shadows lie,
Navigate the midnight sky.
Galaxies in whispers sigh,
Stories told in nebulae.

Planets spin in cosmic dance,
Dreams unfold in sidereal trance.
In the stardust, we advance,
Mysteries of space enhance.

Nebulae in colors blend,
Through the cosmos, we'll ascend.
In the void, the paths extend,
Eternal trails without end.

Starlit maps of ancient lore,
Guide our journey, evermore.
In the heavens we explore,
Wonders found in boundless store.

Astral paths in silence weave,
Every star our hearts deceive.
In the expanse, we believe,
Nebulae, our dreams retrieve.

Midnight Passages

In the hush of midnight's breath,
Silent paths of starlit depth.
Shadows weave a silken weft,
Guiding us from night's behest.

Moonlight spills on cobbled streets,
Whispers of the night entreat.
In the stillness, heartbeats meet,
Echoes of a nocturne sweet.

Midnight's cloak of velveteen,
Covers paths where dreams convene.
Softly tread where dark is seen,
In moon's embrace, serene, serene.

Lantern light in dusky glow,
Marks the way with gentle flow.
Midnight passages we know,
Lead where secrets softly grow.

Under stars, our footsteps blend,
Midnight's passage, journey's friend.
In the dark, no need pretend,
Every path, a story penned.

Luminescent Journeys

Beneath the stars, the pathways gleam,
A shimmered trail of dreams unseen.
We tread on beams of tranquil light,
Guided by the moon's soft sheen.

Through forests deep, where shadows play,
Our steps aligned in night's ballet.
The lanterns of the distant towns,
In whispered echoes gently sway.

With every step, the silver hue,
Embraces whispers in the dew.
As ancient tales in night unfold,
The skies unveil a journey new.

To lands unknown where dreams align,
We chase the glow, the stars define.
Luminescence charts our course,
In cosmic dance, our fates entwine.

The night reveals its secret lore,
In every gleam, a world to explore.
On luminescent journeys vast,
We find the light, forevermore.

Nightlight Travels

Underneath the midnight sky,
We wander where the shadows lie.
With lantern's glow to guide our way,
Through silent streets, we softly sigh.

The whispers of the stars above,
Embrace us with celestial love.
Each step we take on cobblestone,
Becomes a dance, a night-time shove.

Through alleys dark and moonlit lanes,
Our journey weaves, our spirit reigns.
We travel far in dreamlike state,
In search of light where night sustains.

The constellations paint the night,
With patterns of eternal light.
In every twinkle, stories told,
Of voyagers with hearts so bright.

As dawn begins to touch the skies,
Our nightlight travels bid goodbyes.
Yet in our hearts, the journey stays,
A luminous path, where dreams arise.

Twilight Quest

At twilight's hush, the journey starts,
With whispers of the evening's art.
We embark on a quest untold,
Guided by the celestial charts.

The fading sun, a golden hue,
Paints the sky in vibrant blue.
Our steps aligned with dusk's soft glow,
Through twilight's veil, our spirits flew.

In shadows cast by moon's ascent,
We find a peace, a night-time friend.
The stars like jewels in velvet sky,
Mark the path through realms transcend.

Mysteries of the night unfold,
As we traverse through tales of old.
Each step a verse in this grand quest,
In twilight's grasp, we're brave and bold.

As dawn approaches, colors blend,
The twilight's quest draws to an end.
Yet in the embers of the night,
We find new paths, where dreams extend.

Phosphorescent Journeys

In the deep of ocean's night,
Where dreams take flight in silent sight.
We sail on waves of phosphoresce,
Embracing luminescent light.

Beneath the waves, the hidden glow,
Illuminates the depths below.
We journey through the coral's dance,
Enchanted by the ocean's flow.

In caverns deep, where shadows blend,
The light becomes our closest friend.
We uncover secrets long concealed,
In phosphorescent journeys penned.

The creatures of the deep arise,
With tales of ancient seas and skies.
Their luminescence guides our quest,
Through underwater lullabies.

As surface nears, the light subsides,
Yet in our hearts, the glow abides.
Phosphorescent journeys end,
But in our dreams, they'll e'er reside.